Bereft

Bereft

A Story about Love, Loss, and Family

M. A. QUIGLEY

RESOURCE *Publications* • Eugene, Oregon

BEREFT
A Story about Love, Loss, and Family

Copyright © 2022 M. A. Quigley. All rights reserved. Except for brief quotations in critical publications or reviews, no part of this book may be reproduced in any manner without prior written permission from the publisher. Write: Permissions, Wipf and Stock Publishers, 199 W. 8th Ave., Suite 3, Eugene, OR 97401.

Resource Publications
An Imprint of Wipf and Stock Publishers
199 W. 8th Ave., Suite 3
Eugene, OR 97401

www.wipfandstock.com

PAPERBACK ISBN: 978-1-6667-5608-1
HARDCOVER ISBN: 978-1-6667-5609-8
EBOOK ISBN: 978-1-6667-5610-4

12/16/22

For Ben

"He smiled at me, and I desired him like ripples on the ocean making me quiver to my core."

—M.A. Quigley

Never did I think we'd meet
We were free and equal to greet
Though many people wouldn't agree
For years, he was a memory to me
He left me grieving for what
Might have been
Tears of happiness we cried
I thought he was a mirage
And wiped my eyes
"Someone said that you had died."
He looked at me, surprised
"Our family moved away,
We couldn't stand living here
One more day.
We were like prisoners on our land
No one seemed to
Want to understand."
I didn't know what to say
I sighed and breathed on him
My hand clasped in his
Wanting him to feel
Like he belonged
He smiled as we wandered
Along the beach
Where nothing seemed
Out of reach,
We sat talking,
Watching the sunset
I had no regrets
Staying with him that night

The wind sang a lullaby
We camped on the sand
The sea murmured,
Nurturing my heart and mind
Hope visited in my dreams
The sun's rays beamed
Seagulls flapped their wings
Hovering for food
The sea kissed our feet
We walked bereft
Of friends and family
My parents found us
Slapped my back and face,
Through blood and tears,
Nothing had changed
Over the years
Their car flew
To where no happiness grew,
With me in it

***

I opened my diary
Caressing the petals
Of a pressed rose
The smell of it
Lingered on my nose
Remembering him kneeling
Saying he wanted me,
To be his betrothed
"Stop reading," said Mum.
"There are animals that need feeding."
I closed the book and locked it away
To write and read another day
I walked outside throwing pellets
Far and wide
Chooks scratched the earth,
Cackling with their feathers fluttering,
Dogs barked, wagging their tails
Dad arrived in his Ute
Driving me over barren land
I spent the rest of the day shoveling
Digging deep
To put fence posts in
All the while thinking,
About seeing him again
His kisses were the only thing
That could soothe
The broken blisters
On my calloused hands
That was more befitting
On a man

I tossed and turned
Unable to sleep
Seeing visions of him in my mind
Holding me close
Hands lingering on my cheek,
Noses touching, kissing
Wisdom spoke, I closed my eyes
Our community was old with heavy hearts
Gnarled hands from working on the land
Mum expected me to bake bread and cakes
For charities and fetes
Skinning animals, cooking them to eat
I knew that I couldn't stay another day
Mum said I was like an unbridled mare
Because I wouldn't listen to instructions given
She believed he would lead me astray
Galivanting across the countryside
To see one another each day

Later, we met
Walked along the street
Hands clasped
The pulse in our fingers
Beating as one
My parents' sway
Couldn't keep me away
Emotions swept
Through my veins,
I fell into his arms
In the forest just over
We lay in the long grass,
Wilting leaves fell from trees
Flowers closed
While butterflies departed,
No one passing by
We were in harmony
With one another
Falling asleep in tranquillity
Arms encircled around
One another

We woke and lingered
At the river
Winds breathed on it
Making the surface
Spread and quiver
A rainbow of sunlight rose
Above the clouds
Waterfalls burst from mountains
Thundering foam
All over us
As we sailed through
The waterways
Fish flipped and dipped
Slowly we moved
Into the silence
Of the multitudes
Towards a lone cave
He dropped his oars
Helped me step out
We stood in silence
In the cave
Water dripped like a pulse
Stirring deep feelings
In both of us
The wind swept
Deciding to play
Whisking my hair
Around my face

His remorseless heart
was unable to express
Innocence and tenderness
He sought refuge
in his musings
Deceived by someone in childhood
His sorrowful verses,
Lay on the ground
Buried in the water
Lost hopes and desires
No one knew his pain
He was one of nine children
Believing he had nothing to gain,
Jeweled dreams inspired
Filling him with passion and fire
He woke but his dreams didn't transpire
Sorrow encapsulated him forevermore
I tried to comfort and console him
But his mind switched gears
Wanting to leave
I viewed him with shock and surprise,
Like a small flame that turns into a bushfire
He rowed us back to the shore
Leaving me there filled with scorn
I walked home, lay on my bed,
In the morning, watered and fed
Outside, I walked through fields of ripening corn
When I'd finished all my chores,
I went to the beach

I sat on the shore of the tempestuous sea
My heart ached
No one in my family offered any sympathy
I walked for miles and saw him
Sitting by a campfire
My mind tormented by hope and dread
Tears streamed down my face
Hand half raised in a wave,
He came to greet me,
Murmuring an apology
Which was sweet to taste
We lay on the sand
The sun shining between the clouds
His eyes were proud, giving hope
For a moment, all was calm
The silent sea, a soothing balm,
But I could not help but fear
Hell, and hatred languished near

The shades of evening
Wrapped around us
Beaming auburn
We waded into the sea
Splashing one another
Free to dive or swim
Our footprints showed in the sand
As we walked, holding hands
The ocean quivered
The sea lapped upon the shore
Caressing our thoughts
He turned to me and closed his eyes
I knew that he was smitten

Our veins wound their way like a stream
Along a field of uneven terrain,
With flowers growing everywhere,
Their beauty and fragrance emanating
There was no death, only love
No light obscured the two of us
Our souls burned brightly
Breathing in each other and our surrounds
Our hearts beating fast
Warmed by this wondrous sight,
On a cold winter's night

***

We met at the cave
Living in a pretend world
Away from prying eyes
Snatching each moment
Like we were going to die
We sat huddled together
Listening to a song
Floating through the air,
Wild music lapping at the cave's feet
Spreading into the darkness deep
A bird flew out from a nest
Her hatchlings followed put to the test
Rising high and lowering,
Before the next rush of music hollowing,
His hands circled my waist
Face smiling, fading to a sad gaze,
Foreheads touching, saying nothing
The curve of the moon waning
The shadow of the fire hissing
Silhouetting us against the walls
Nerves moved like a tick in his veins
Our noses touched and our lips parted, kissing
My fingers gently caressed his face
Like a harpist playing
Our emotions like a well
Full to overflowing
While the trees outside groaned and cracked,
I walked home alone at sunrise

My ideas swirled like a tornado
As I took each step,
Knowing I wouldn't be met,
With joy and merriment
My soul flared when I saw home
My parents' teeth gnawed and gnashed
As they spoke,
Mocking me for what I'd done
We weren't rich or poor but proud
Mum said aloud
I should leave him
Because he wasn't like us
My head churned and swiveled
From one parent to the other
Their argument oozed like puss
From an open wound festering,
I couldn't understand
Why they were making such a fuss
Happy visions came to mind
Each time I commented,
Mum said I was blind

After breakfast, I rubbed my eyes,
Smoothed my hair down
Twirling around in a new dress
"What madness," said Mum.
"Never try to impress anyone."
She shoved a bucket
And gumboots in my hands
"Get to work, there are chores to be done
Before you go out having fun."
My eyes shone with love and angst
I took the dress off, changed
Jumped on the Ute
Wheels skidded on gravel
Dust whirled around in the air
Muck flew off my pitchfork over the land
I thought of us dancing, holding hands
Wanting the time to go fast,
So, we could be together again

Dreaming; eyes flickering,
Like watching a motion picture
Minutes and hours crept
My empty heart, desolate
Frozen tears like glaciers
Casting a doubtful hue
Across the briars
Moss grew on rough walls
Of the cave
Where we met to sit,
And talk another day
While the town ebbed and flowed,
We remained unchanged
His voice was low, almost unheard
Murmuring like music
Lips on mine, melting my tears
And icy heart, free of pain
We breathed as one
I smiled and held my head high
Our spirits were like flowers
Touched by the wind, harmonizing
Upon wakening,
There was no release or respite
Everyone judged us,
We weren't meant to be
Despite our families
No one sought to understand
Our relationship had no appeal
Because we weren't the same color

***

Gentle rains came on dry plains
Sweeping the dust away
The crops grew, but there was nothing new
To talk about
Money flew down from the sky
My parents rejoiced in their bounty
He arrived one night
"Go away," said Dad.
"Sir, no one can tame my feelings
Like a fireball shining bright,
I have for your daughter."
Dad laughed in his face,
"You're a disgrace
You will never be able to afford her,
You are someone we mistrust,
You're not good enough
For our daughter."
Dad slammed the door
I ran outside, reached for my love's arm
Making him turn around,
Fury showed on his face
Like thunder and lightning bursting
Through the sky
My fingertips gently
Touched his cheek
His eyes undressed me
We nuzzled, eyes lowered,
The back of his hand moving
Gently down my arm,
Creating shivers to my core

Dad stormed toward us
Pushed us apart
Shoving him out the gate,
I wrote in my diary
My fingers bled, cutting
Into the page with my pen,
When would their hatred end?
The whole scenario depressed me
Eerie shadows played
On my bedroom wall
The curtain swept over my hair
Like a ghost scaring me
I pulled the window shut
The verbal abuse my love copped
Was oil poured on my soul,
Staining my heart and mind with sadness

Mum said I had many choices,
And asked why I picked him
Dad said I was living in sin,
"No daughter of mine is going to marry him."
He slapped me once, if not twice
Told me to come to my senses
Or I'd get into strife
I refused to listen, crept out of the house
Found my love near the cave
My heart was helpless
I was like a stray dog wanting love
I leaned against him on the beach
His hands were like a thousand voices
Caressing my soul with their language
The unicorn moon's rays shone on us
He gave me hope, making me calm as the sea
The hungry hours were like a tiger
Chasing prey away
We wandered into the cave
Danced holding hands
Firelight created shapes
Filling us with warmth and pleasure
The breath between his lips
Sweet as honey
Sent from heaven to taste
But he felt like an outcast,
Abandoned and alone
I wanted to take him home,
Plead with my parents for him to stay
What is love if we can't have our way?

He trembled and said he didn't
Want to be their slave
He wanted to build a house
To live with me—not alone
And I felt safe

From the deep recesses of his caresses,
He refused to think about his parents
Took an extra job like no other
Beliefs floated above his head
Like grey clouds threatening rain,
Grapevines fluttered in their trellised lines
I watched him pick and stomp on them
Later he walked stooped, back bent
Like an old man
Soon he knew he would have to decide
I hoped he wouldn't hurt my pride
Leave them and come with me
They laughed at what he'd done
And he resigned when the sunset
They wouldn't let him forget
What a fool he'd been
Elders taught him to paint
Telling stories about the Dreamtime
Conjuring serpents, spirits, and animals
Over a blank page
His imagination captivated everyone
Around the town, making them proud
Painting stories night and day
They said he was obscene and blind
To think he could be a love of mine
From the deep abyss of wonder and bliss,
He made a lot of money

***

I sat in a pew with my parents
No sign of my love
A storm raged in my heart
Filled with reproach and doubt
Lamenting, saying a reluctant prayer
No faith in God that he would listen
The priest had a penetrating presence
He raised his voice in the incensed air
Saying to love thy neighbor is divine
My triumphant soul harmonized
Bursting with joy, like music sent from heaven
God shone through the stained glass
A spectacular gleam
And I knew I was forgiven

Afterwards, we met at the beach
I told my love what the priest had preached
His eyes narrowed like I was telling lies
He said, "Church talks of hell where someone
Walks on hot coals with blistered feet
Not about loving people you meet
We can't go on this way."
He left me wounded as a lion
Torn to shreds in a fight
Crimson with its heart ripped out
From a predator late at night
I pleaded with him not to leave
But he pushed my hands
Muttered something under his breath
Leaving me weeping, feeling bereft
I wanted the lapping sea to take me away

No pity, release, or respite
I rode the waves of ruin
Spiralling, sinking
Into a bottomless void
No one to guide about lost love or life
Darkness, no light
"One day, you'll make a farmer
A happy wife," said Mum.
I wept while she smiled
My hidden opinions each worse
Than the last, exhausted me
Like a worn record needle
No sweet music to sound
Just static pain piercing my heart

I believed deep inside
He hadn't changed his mind
His parents kept his idle hands busy,
As did mine
To look at us, you'd think we'd changed
Mum said my love was like a magician,
Hypnotizing
She could see through our disguise
And just to spite
Organized a date with my neighbor
On the farm over, who was looking for a wife
I refused to go, "He's not my type."
"We don't care," she said.
"You'll do as you're told
Just be polite."

I ran outside; I had to flee
I hated my parents
Treating me like a slave
If I stayed any longer,
I'd go insane
All hope for my future torn aside
In my eyes, we were equal, him and I
Mum yelled, "Come back here."
But I kept walking
I was tired of her interfering
My feet riveted to the earth
Peering at him, fishing by the river,
Leaving his line resting on a branch
He was gentle and wise,
Came over to me, apologizing
Which made me dizzy with delight
My spirit floated upwards
Like a lotus flower, opening
Leaving the murky recesses behind

***

I stood against the wall
Like a flower budded, tall
In the kitchen waiting
To attend the town hall ball
My dress, yellow as a daisy,
Tightly budded
My parents were like cats licking cream
Their eyes couldn't conceal their gleam
When a farmer's son arrived,
His eyes flashed up and down
Resting on my cleavage
We drove in silence to the ball
Inside, he saw someone he knew
Leaving me to wither
While people danced
Like puppets with forced smiles,
I stepped outside and viewed my love
Standing behind a tree,
We strode off into the woods,
Twirling around under nature's hood,
My dress opened like it was in full bloom
As we danced in the deepest, darkest place,
Hidden away from prying eyes
Someone called out my name
Wanting me to run, heel, and sit
But I was used to their tricks
Like a disobedient animal, was what I'd become
No one could pull me, push me, pick me up,
Or beg me to do as they said

My mind was larger than ten men
We stayed and bathed in the moonlight

***

Ripe as a mango
Face sparkling like a diamond,
Hair shimmering like snow
Smile, bigger than the universe
I couldn't wait to tell him,
I was carrying his child
Knowing he'd rejoice because it was ours
I led him into the cave to watch the sunset
Where darkness descended,
Lighting a candle
Flame hovering, creating a shadow
Waiting for the right moment
His eyes were like a fish, his face agape
His hands moved over his chin
Like he was asking himself,
How to get out of the predicament he was in,
He noticed me watching him and held me close
"That's wonderful news," he said. "I'm stoked."

***

We sat on the couch kissing
His parents arrived home early
Their voices hissed and whipped
Wounding me
I trembled when I spoke
"Why do you want to torture me,
When we are so much in love?" I croaked.
For which they laughed
Pushed us apart
My love said nothing
He was a mouse caught in a trap
Eaten alive by two feral cats
Neither of us could tame

His parents thought he had shamed them
Unwilling to listen, abominating
Later, they came with him, to my house
No compromise
His head bent with lament
Sad eyes unwilling to look at mine
We both knew we wouldn't stay apart
He was doing what they'd asked
They were bloodhounds growling, huge and grim
Ripping and tearing at my flesh,
Refusing to get to know me
My heart stabbed with swords, puncturing
I was deaf to their despair
I ran inside and saw Mum
Watching them through the living room blinds
Dad came out of the barn
Waving his arms, shooing them
"Get off my property, go away."
I lay on my bed reading my love's poetry,
A sweet melody in my brain
In amongst our parents' gloom,
Our love did bloom

We were an overexposed photo
A disease ate our image
Called parents
Paralyzing us
Nowhere to go
Best to lie low
The telephone was off the hook
No one could call
They were acting like brutes
I struggled to breathe
Didn't want to eat
The photo was getting fainter
Dad scolded me, "Stop acting coy,
You'll find no joy with him,
And you'll be hated."
His comments stung
Like a bee sting swelling inside
Hurting my pride
I learned to ignore him
My love fulfilled my innermost thoughts
I blushed when I saw him
Like a sinner, caught
But didn't God forgive everyone?
I refused to listen
To everyone's snide remarks
Or care about their scorn
He left me daydreaming
But Dad had other ideas
He grabbed my arm

"Get out of bed, do your chores
There are animals
That need to be fed."

At night, mute walls spoke
Their voices foamed
And raged like swells
Filled with desperation and hate
I didn't think I could live
Under my parents' roof
For another day
So, I packed my bags and waited
Until it was late
Not caring when I would see them again
Through the mist of the night,
An image rose by the open-curtained window
My love's eyes were soft as the wind
He held my hand, and I climbed out
We ran away like two phoenixes

He was a son, someone's child
Not a beast like my parents had said
A troubled face I knew and loved
We sat upon the bridge like two birds calling
Watching the river receding and flowing
I rested in his feathers
The crescent moon above the trees
Created an eerie harmony
We were lost in the silence and solitude
Throwing stones, making them pool and dip
We took off our clothes and went for a swim

Wrinkled skin, like dried prunes
Two old friends, no towels
Our damp clothes clung to us
But we didn't care
Because we were having fun
We lay on the grass
Dawn blew out the moon's lantern wick
And the sun dried us

He caught a fish
Scaled it clean
Made a fire
We sat on the earth
Listening to birds
Chirping in the trees
Eating cooked, soft meat
Talking about our future
Away from town
Moving where people would accept us
No one would frown
Or put us down

At night, I dreamed
Of a candle flame,
The color of persimmon
Lighting the way forth
With one windy bellow,
The wick snuffed
We walked like blind children
Holding onto one another,
Trying to steady our feet,
Free falling off a precipice into quicksand,
Howling and yelling
Bleeding hearts,
Our eyes on one another
As we took our last breath,
Making me wake, distressed

Mum saw me in the street
She glanced at me
I could tell she was peeved
Pushing me into the car
Driving me home
Scenarios rippled
Like the wind on the sea
Making me shudder
But later that night
My mind was an umbilical cord
Winding its way to him,
I opened the back door,
Walked out the gate
We met by the river
I fed on his soul as he did on mine
Knowing what he'd say,
Before he opened his mouth,
Keeping to ourselves
When other people were around,
A nod, a tap on the knee
The way our eyes moved
Our hands caressed the crease
On one another's backs
We communicated in silence
Even when we were alone
We starred in our own motion-picture show

Part of the old me died that night
He was the one who knew my plight
Drawn to me like the sun,
When dark fades to light
The air grew calm,
We sat in amongst the dunes
Watching the fishermen
Creating intrigue and mystery in the fog
As something moved up from the depths
Pulling a line in, leaving us agog
We ran into the deep recesses of the cave,
I slowly turned to him, cuddling
Our voices reverberated like the draught
We slept in one another's arms
Waking to the breeze
Playing soft music in the reeds,
The glittering eye shadow sky
Drawing dark mascara lines
And the sand scattering millions of notes
Around us

We walked along the shore
Joy faded from his face
My frenzied song
Lost its way and his lips fed on mine
Whispering words, I cannot repeat,
We strode inside the cave
Watching a storm out at sea
On the rocks, a seagull landed
In a chatty mood
The sea's music boisterous around us
The rain dried up like a summer's day
We made our way to the shore
Stepped into a boat
Not knowing where
The waves would take us

***

In an empty church
My stomach lurched
Remembering the last time
I'd been to mass
I thought God wouldn't be kind to us
A statue of Mary, pale and worn
I stood at the altar surrounded by flowers
That smelt like death in someone's final hour
Frankincense burned, and we lit two candles
Placed them in the altar rails
His hand in mine, walking side by side
Threadbare carpet moved beneath our feet
Floorboards creaked and groaned
As a tear trickled down my cheek,
We knelt in a rosewood pew
Viewing the rainbow sea
Through the stained glass
Lighting up the room
Bending our heads, palms together,
Closing our eyes
I heard him breathing,
The warmth of his body next to mine
Hoping God was with us listening,
That he'd forgive me for loving someone
Whom my parents despised

Mum thought she knew what was right
Preaching about the Catholic faith
Saying grace
Sinning like everyone else
Stealing neighbors' flowers
Trying to strike them in her garden
She said God listened
To everyone's prayers and he cared
Like no one else does
But God was deaf to mine
Like a stray cat, disobedient,
Wanting to give and receive love
I lacked both, I needed someone
To listen and obey, not lead me astray
I'd done enough,
I didn't want to be assessed

My footprints were invisible
Like I'd grown two wings
Unwilling to descend
Emotions left buried in the church
Mum was right
God spoke to me in my heart and mind
His eyes sent love through mine
I knew I was doing the right thing
Being with this love of mine

We sat under a tree
The sun caressing us
In the warm shade,
The smell of cut grass
And hay mingled
The wind teased leaves,
Making them shake
While animals mated,
Filled with hope and love
The tender pulse of each day trembled
Bringing a new life to fill the world
Rain caressed the earth,
And our love was fluid like a lake
Calm, deep, and serene
Floating day by day, no waves
Blue skies hypnotizing
No more showers of God's tears,
Or angry storms
I wanted a house
With our children living in it

Our minds and bodies were antipodes
The creek was a marble, mirroring
Turning us both upsides down
Like mind and thought swimming deep,
Unwilling to let go, suffocating in our sorrow
Even when we slept and woke,
No joy, only lament
We got our wish,
And no one wanted to know us
We wandered through life
He failed to make me his wife
We had nowhere to go

My stomach grew
My breasts were small melons
Alas, there was no baby
To rock and sing to in my arms
Blood trickled down my inner thighs
Weeping for what might have been
We sat on the beach that night
Hugging each other tight
Making me believe everything would be okay
Mum said my assumptions were lame
She failed to tame
Wild hormones raging
An internal battle
For which there was no intelligence or glory

Birds sang in the trees
Their sweet melody failed
To soothe our hearts and minds
As we walked to the beach,
We sat by the seaside
Watching the waves roll in,
The madness of its tone sank all around us
Across the sky, suffering black,
And red like hell
Even though I believed in God,
Free will and destiny
I had my pride, but my true love was blind
Looking towards the darker side,
Worried about his parents
Old and frail, unrelenting
The sway and pull got too much
His morals played a different tune
Which no longer serenaded me
Jarring words hurt my ears
About how he loved them
We hardly spoke
The rain mourned with me
Scattering tears across the sand,
His eyes glistened
Pleading for me to understand
I left him there, stood up,
And walked toward home
Because there was nowhere else to go
I became invisible
Melding with grey buildings

In the town's streets, the words he said
Gave me no appetite
I lay upon a concrete step
I wanted God to give me a sign
Like an ethereal glow,
The moon hid, angering me
I believed I would never see my love again
He would sail alone through life
When they died
My cheeks quivered
I wanted to talk to him
Make him see sense
Later, I knocked on his door, dripping wet,
Shivering
I prayed he'd ask me in
He stood gazing at me
His mute face spoke
My tears chased my denial and naivety
I stared up at the rage in the sky
Swallowed my pride
And walked back home alone

Abandoned like a shipwreck,
My parents were wild dogs
Tearing my head apart
Telling me how to behave
I was a young lady out of college,
Not allowed to love a beast
But I knew more than them
My mind churned,
Insomnia set in
Wings fanned inside my chest
Wanting to take flight
From all that was supposed to matter

In my dreams, he couldn't keep away
Lured by lust and mothering
His arms enclosed me, smothering
My eyes were ice blocks, melting
My hormones were a caged lion roaring
I opened the door
And he flew out of the room
Like a bird escaping from its cage
Flying high out of sight,
Alphabet soup formed boys' names
My breasts expressed frothy milk
No one to drink
No heart beating
The air was too thick to breathe
I woke up screaming
"Won't someone help me, please?"
But no one came to my aid

***

After my chores
I walked back to the cave
My mind was in a daze
A fur rug lay
Near the entrance
I called out his name
Creating stories
Which he starred in
Repulsing me, how could I
Believe the lies he'd said?
Telling me what I wanted to hear
Birds babbled and dispersed
The sea roared
My heart turned to snow
He'd done a rogue's act
Like eggs just hatched and cracked
Watched by a cat,
Ready to pounce, salivating
The wind sneered
Now I was the cat
I sharpened my claws
Tail in the air
Flicking back and forth
When I saw him
Green eyes flouncing about
Shredding the rug
Urinating
"Don't try to feed me
My favorite food
I'm not in the mood," I said.

I ran along the shore
Through the forest
Back home to bed
Tossing and turning
Unable to sleep
All I could do was weep

Later, I did see him
His limbs shook
Sad, meek face, brown bleary eyes
I knew he'd been crying
His voice was icy cold
Lips trembling on a sunny day,
He carried an enormous chain
Which weighed him down to the ground
His arms reaching out for mine
I pulled back and hesitated
Wanting to turn and runaway
My mind and soul
Tormented with disappointment,
mistrust, and unhappiness
Fog covered the road ahead
I didn't care if his parents had died
In a car accident late at night
I no longer yearned for his hugs, masks
And painted faces
My soul crumbled when he spoke
About a new future for us
He left me gasping
For the tiniest molecule of air

An algae wave leaped high,
Covering us everywhere
My hair stuck to my face
I must've looked hideous
My clothes were dripping
Like I was hung out to dry
But he wasn't fastidious
He stuttered and his body shook
His words swam and sank
He picked up a shell and held it to his ear
Like he was listening to a loved one near
The wind hissed and bellowed
I wore a mask with a compassionate face
Put my arm around his waist
His head rested on my shoulder
like a pillow
I walked with him back to his house
Sympathizing with his grief-stricken strain
His body and mind
Overloaded with pain
His voice was a violin playing
An unyielding tune
On a gloomy day
He waited while I showered
And changed
Walking back home with me

My love didn't grow
Like a tree in the snow
Heavy-laden but with a glow
My razored tongue
Sawed through the wood
Words like splinters
Flying thick and fast,
Until it became blunt,
Not from overuse
But from the truth,
Words I thought I'd never say
His mouth agape
I did not move,
Standing tall and resolute,
He used to walk
With his chest out, proud
His eyes flickered like candles
On a birthday cake
Which was no longer sweet to taste
But he didn't leave me feeling empty
I was full of knowledge
Like I'd eaten plenty

Purple mouth
A stain from a kiss
From which I'm not proud
Lacerations and ulcers
Unable to eat or drink
A searing pain burst through
Like his lies
Making me cry
Listening to his howling throng,
Pulling me close to him,
Wanting to kiss my blood,
But I no longer wanted
To be polluted by his tongue
Dad pitied me with his gentle eyes
I sat and listened to his diatribe
"He is no prince charming,
As you believed
He has led you astray
There are many fish in the sea,
But they swim deep
Your trampled heart will mend
You will find someone
To love again
Don't sit around and mope for him,
Or think about revenge
Wipe your eyes, don't cry
If he calls, I'll tell a lie and say,
That you're not home."
But I wailed and cussed
Behind closed doors

The flame in my heart
Flickered back and forth
In the morning, it was no more
Like something had died inside me

My eyes were covered with a veil
Our hearts had mingled as one
Now, the veil flew off my face
My fresh eyes viewed him with disgrace
At my front door, looking forlorn,
What did I see in this man?
I vowed not to be deceived again,
Even when he begged,
Pleading like a poor man in the street
Jiggling a tin with coins, so he could eat
He was poison in a cup
I refused to drink from anymore
He lent toward my lips for a kiss,
And I recoiled
He professed his love for me that day
Asked me what was wrong,
But I couldn't say
I'd heard it all before
Like Mum said to Dad
When he said things
That made her mad
Even though he was my first crush
I asked him to go away,
My heart reduced to mush
When I said I never wanted to see him again,
A dejected look crossed his face,
Eyes welling, opening his mouth,
But Dad came up and yelled, "get out,"
Slamming the door behind him.

I sat and wept after he'd left
Licking my wounds like a kitten
Somewhere in my heart and mind, still smitten
"Stop crying," said Mum.
"There will be more men
You'll find someone you adore—
A farmer on a station like your Dad."
The thought of it made me sad
I buried my emotions for them not to take hold
I lay down on my bed and slept
In my dreams, I wept like a tidal wave
Drowning me

Outside, I viewed the starlit sky
Prayed to heaven
With an icy heart,
Filled with spears
That wouldn't come out
"God, I'm tapping on your door
Let me in!
Let me in!
I've had enough of living on earth
Speak to me, don't abandon me tonight
I want to hear your voice
Telling me everything will be alright."
I walked back inside
There was no light
I stumbled and fell like I was blind

My legs moved
Like a person on crutches
I stared in the mirror
A sorrowful face greeted me
As I brushed my hair into place,
Mascara bled down my face,
My body hunched over
When I was behind closed doors,
I punched the mirror
The glass shattered like ice
Blood dripped from my knuckles
I let out a shriek that sounded like a chuckle
Leaving me stunned
What had I done?
Who was this person?
Surely, not me

Voices echoed, all-around
Creating an other-worldly sound
The sun burnt my skin
And changed it to another color
My mind was in a chasm
Where nothing could be fathomed
No emotion, or smiling face
My words had no power
I opened my mouth
And stuttered for hours
Like I was wearing summer clothes
On an icy day

Invisible scars covered my body
As it moved through life,
People called me beautiful
If they only knew
How battered and bruised
I was on the inside
The past played a movie,
In my mind's eye
Which flittered each scene to life,
I couldn't find the pause, delete
Or off button to stop it
I cut my arm for relief
Blood burst and dripped
Making me breathe out a heavy sigh

***

I flew a kite; it wandered free
While I lay on the grass,
In the park at noon
My mind drifted
Holding on tight
To the unraveling string
The kite wavered in the wind
Bobbing, dodging, ducking
Like a missile attacking
Remembering how we were
In full flight
No one cared about the two of us
But individually they made too much fuss
Why couldn't we be like the string
And the kite
Roaming around carefree?

His love letters were like buried treasure
Found under my pillow, in my bag, or pockets
Sending my heart soaring like a rocket
Now I read them over again
The promises fell off each page
My lips trembled at the lies and deceit
The snake in the grass had slithered away
I lit a match and burned each letter
No longer soiled by the serpent's tongue
Each word floated into the ether one-by-one
Cleansing my soul and mind

Dreams of ruin
Lingered above my pillow
The sea rocked and a storm came
I failed to get out of bed
My ship had sunk
I was drenched in anguish, thinking of him
No longer looking forward to tomorrow
Lightning laughed at my plight
Trying to reach me under
The depths of the sea
But I had fallen in too deep
I lay upon the ocean floor
Unwilling to flee
No hope
No love
No atmosphere
No one to hold me near
My destiny crushed
I slept for hours
No consolation, tormented by the truth
Frozen like a glacier
Which refused to move and flow
My world had become a kaleidoscope of woe
No music serenading my ears
The record stuck
Static filled the void
Fish stared at me with big wide eyes
And a dark shadow loomed over me

Love died, Dad was wise
My love's words had betrayed me
I was a rose picked and spent
No longer heaven scent,
Decayed, unwilling to show my face,
Not wanting to see anyone that day
My heart filled with grief and shame
My thorns were sharp, penetrating
Deep within my wounded soul,
Dad made me go into town
People whispered and pointed, sneering
I bowed my head, fled, and wept
Unaware I'd left my groceries
On the supermarket step

The rain was a balm
Soothing me
I lived in hope
But now, I'd sunk
Into a deep abyss
Staying in bed
With the curtains drawn
Feeling forlorn
Mum dragged me out of bed
Made me get dressed
But I was disheveled
I dragged my body
Through each day
Not caring what anyone
Had to say
One morning, I woke
My emotions were clear
No longer weighed down
My wings were huge, soft, and swift
A calmness swept over me
Like a river at night
Where campers find
Peace and harmony

My beliefs about him
Were laid to rest
I walked alone
Hard hearts, weights of stone
Would never forgive me
Nor I, them
For what they had said
And the way they'd treated me
They couldn't see
The error of their ways
For all the blame
They'd pushed upon me
About shaming them
Because of the way I'd acted
And what I'd done
"Couldn't you see
I was in love?" I said.
They growled and snarled
Like hungry wolves
"What would you know about love?
You're too young," said Mum.
"That's right, I forgot
You know everything," I said.
"Don't talk like that to your Mum,"
Said Dad and whacked me over the head.
I stood and wept
Breathing in vain
Gasping at what had become
Of my family

Wisdom smiled one sun-filled day
He made a call and said,
He'd suffered enough
And believed I had too
Wanting to meet
Where we could have
Something to eat
Our broken chain
Became a necklace
Where seeds grew ripe fruit,
Changes occurring from pain to bliss
Moving, breathing, no one to tell
Mum found out
And said I would go to hell
Hands moved over my smooth skin
Self-love, talking, did anyone hear?
No acknowledgement from anyone near
My eyes were like a liquid sky
When a neighbor came over
And said my love had died
He was king hit and stabbed in a fight
A tornado of emotions screeched
Through my soul,
My body whirled around, I fell on the floor
I woke to contempt and loathing
On human brows
"What have I done wrong?" I said aloud.
Arms folded over my chest,
Nuns hovered like I was about to be given
My last rites and laid to rest

He came to me as a memory in a dream
Bowing his head
Like a flower shadowed by pine trees,
With wounded frost-bitten limbs
His voice was faint, intoxicating
Like his smell emanating,
The sun's rays changed and set,
Into night
I couldn't articulate what he'd said
His roots shriveled
I could tell he was troubled
I woke and lo and behold,
Someone phoned and said,
He'd died calling out my name

I was a grey cloud ready to burst its load
Hiding behind my sunglasses
The wind was singing a foul tune
Which harmonized with the gloom
A crow sat on the church spire
And through the wilderness of my mind,
I could see no reprise
No open casket to view him once more
I stood at the back of the church near the door
Watching men in black suits walking heel-to-toe
Lifting his dead body skywards,
Haltering voices singing a hymn,
All the while wondering,
If God had forgiven him, for his sins
Stepping outside before anyone else
Feeling like a voodoo doll stuck with pins

My love's death was like a fish
With a hook in its mouth
Searing with pain at its demise
Wanting to dive back into the river,
But all it could do was flip, flop, and flap
While trying to breathe one last time,
There was no moaning at its agony
Like there was none with mine

At the wake
Drunk and withdrawn
Feeling forlorn
Sitting in a pub
Noisy banter
Glasses clinking
Lots of drinking
Music playing out-of-kilter
Trying to fill a void
There was no radiance outside
For the moon's globe
Had blown tonight
I staggered and fell
Like a newborn foal,
Found a seat on a city street
And fell asleep until the morning hours

Troubled skies
Stained my heart and mind
With paint bleeding like a well,
Full to overflowing
Clothes bursting
Wet straw stuck to my face
I was like a scarecrow
In a field of my own making
My parents viewed me with disgrace
Squawking like crows
Heaping abuse on me

***

Shouting, moaning, groaning,
Sweating, panting, screaming,
Listening to a newborn crying
Self-consumed sparks of love and hope
The fire's embers died; ashes fluttered,
Leaving lemons in my mouth
A whirlpool of thoughts,
My body jerking forward, head down
Fading into nothing when the needle came out

Moving in slow motion, no one listened
Confined to my room
Wicked shapes entered
Savages filled with ghostly pride,
Nowhere to hide
No warmth or tenderness
Their tongues wagging back and forth
Dictating, not free from guilt or pain
My mask had gone again
My soul remained left wanting
For a bundle taken away
At dawn

Hope spoke to me in my sleep
Wings soft and rapid as thought,
Silent glow of morning beams
Hours chased the day
Like a wounded emu, bleeding
Trying to stay upright, willing itself to move
My task was done
I was poked and prodded
Told to work, cook, and clean
Through my tears, hopes, and fears
My spirit was no longer calm
Farmers came and went
But there was no merriment
On my days off, I sat on the grass
Where tightly budded flowers grew
Birds flew into a canopy,
Eating and regurgitating food
To feed their hatchlings
As ink consumed the sky,
And it was my dinnertime

***

I had no preconceptions
In this life, I lived
Halting breath as I meditated
My mind was a grey slate
I knew he'd be waiting
For me behind the gate
When I reached heaven
It wouldn't be too late
We could still be together
Until then, I'd live my life in isolation
The shrink said I was delusional
But I couldn't deny these feelings
I had locked inside
I thrust and wailed
She said I was cheating myself
Of a good life
"Here, take this pill, it will calm
Your heart and mind
And keep you quiet."

His spirit hid behind a cloud
A dark, calamitous film
In the windless air
Fluid darkness with ethereal pearly white
Shining forth like snow
Illuminating the fields, river, and sea
Where we used to go
Graphic arrows added brightness to the sky
He bellowed with a drum roll
From up high
Creating joy, delight, and madness
Making dogs howl, running inside
I stood outside, witnessing his music
Caressed by his tears, outpouring
My lips moving, murmuring,
Matters of the heart
Until now, I couldn't let go

Colors woven through my eyes
Red, yellow, blue, and green
Take on different hues when mixed
With anger, jealousy, depression, and hate
Like a prism, intermingled on the wall dilate
The one I wanted and needed was love
A color blended with God's heart
For which we are all a part,
But I don't feel he's within reach
God must be too busy
To listen to me

I was fragile
Since my love died
Losing him hurt me
And wounded my pride
My eyes lit up
My hair was in place
I smiled like a doll
Nodded my head up and down
Left and right
I didn't have any appetite
Weightless as a dragonfly
As I moved through life,
Keeping my mouth shut
Not wanting to do anything wrong
My passion died
The lights turned off
Inside an abandoned house
Where no one wanted to live
And had moved on or died

At night, I sat under a tree
Asking heaven
If it had any messages for me
Ants marched around my feet
Crickets sang as the sky wept
My brain was overladen with questions
Left unanswered
We were polarized opposites
Him in paradise, me here
Wanting him to hold me near
A mist made my pallid skin glow,
But my stamen has turned to mold
A bird moved into the canopy above
And the moon eclipsed, turning red
"Morph into something; let me know
You are here."
Rain tapped on the ground
Like morse code
I listened to its music
Serenading my soul
And went inside to bed

I was a drop of dew
In the universe
Sparkling
Tender to touch
Wet like a kiss,
That lingered long
As sweet as candy
To taste and smell
Fragile as a baby
That had just been born
All I wanted
Was to be loved and adored
Now my life was filled
With heartache and forlorn

***

Being with him
In a dream
I slept and rose
Our beliefs flowed
Like a stream
Melding heaven and earth
His sweet breath caressed my neck
Arousing my senses
Whispering he was sorry
For all that he'd done

I sat in the cave one last time
In the deep recesses of her dwelling,
Stored with a treasure of birds nesting,
The sea playing a symphony and my breathing
She listened and wept,
Her tears dripping and pooling,
She never slept, all the while witnessing
If I were younger, I would be frightened
And want to flee, but sound and memory
Provided comfort, familiarity
Moving pictures formed on her walls
The earthy odor reminded me
Of our walks by the river,
Bare feet wandering through the muddy grass

Outside, an array of stars
Outshone the waning moon
The restless tide frothed and fumed
I wanted it to whisk me away
In the breeze, my cotton dress
Was an open umbrella
Dancing to its tune
The sand attacked like it was fighting
An unseen force
Cutting into my flesh
I ran towards the road and headed north
All was quiet on the streets
Not an animal or human I did meet
I stumbled in my haste,
And stopped to rest

His voice spoke to me
Whispering in a vivid dream
I could smell him
Touch his skin
Like I was standing
In front of him
The birds sang in the trees
I heard him whispering
Romantic overtones, silence
The present choked the past
His black curly hair
Bounced around his face,
In the masquerading moon
I woke crying,
Stumbling, stopping
Like a city tram propping
Not wanting to go home

No humans for miles around
Heard a sound
When Mum gasped for air
And fell on the floor in the house
The sheep, cows, rabbits, dogs, and chickens
Stood silent for a moment, listening
Walking around once again,
Dad put a nail in a fence
To section off an open space
Unaware a tragedy had taken place,
He found her hours later
Called out to me,
But I was like a nomad wandering free
Nowhere to be seen
I saw dust fly
Heard a siren blare
But it was too late
Because she was no longer there
Her spirit free
Dad cursed and cussed
Making a huge fuss
Because he couldn't find me
"Your Mum's dead,
You should've been here," he said.
Like it was all my fault

Standing at the church door
Watching Mum for the last time
Looking like an actor
Lying asleep
Covered in makeup
My eyes were like sun-kissed dew
As I sat in a pew and bowed my head
Trying to comprehend
That she was dead
I said a silent prayer
Later, I sat on the ground
Beside her mound
In amongst the grass and flowers
Reading cards on it for hours
I visited her each day
Nothing could keep me away
Each night I lay awake in pain
To speak of my grief
I didn't dare
No one would listen
No one would care

For years, my arctic eyes shed no tears
Sitting in a psychologist's chair
Paying an enormous fee
Wanting Mum to be with me,
Then one sunny day my tears fell
Like water poured into a wishing well,
I still dwell upon my memories
And the day she left me
I am older than she was back then
Her spirit I have seen
Albeit in a dream when she visits me

Unable to sleep
Out into the cemetery, I creep
Fearful I'd wake the dead
Radiance filled the void
Between heaven and earth
I sat upon Mum's grave
Gold words glared, I could see our names
Spelled out and her age
Why did she have to die so young?
Gargoyles and angels witnessed me
Weep and sigh
There was chaos in the scrub nearby
A cacophony of leaves in the trees
Something dropped and scurried
A bird called; a rabbit stopped mid-hop
Running, burrowing
Fireflies flashed
I trembled in the cold, not knowing what to say
Dad didn't know what I lacked
The universe went on minding its business
And her death seemed inconspicuous

The air was like a tonic; I breathed in and out
Unwilling to eat, dropping to my knees,
A vision hovered in front of me
With two large wings, no feet
Her gown flowed around her in the wind
The skin on my arms and legs bristling
I closed my eyes and opened them again
Her gaze glued to mine
She wore a tight-lipped smile
As she soared out of sight,
Spreading ash all over the countryside
No one was in the field witnessing
I stayed awake, fog enveloping me
Making me blend in with the scenery

The sun laid a hand on my forehead, waking me
I blamed myself for everything
Wanted to die
My head was a chatterbox criticizing
I sat on the ground meditating
Imagining my body levitating,
Free from the house my soul lived in,
Which was liberating
The night nursed my thoughts
Did I dream or imagine the phoenix?
Or was it a message from above?
My mind reflected on the sky
One thing I knew for certain:
The vision was Mum

Dad slurred his words
He was like a hung man
Mum murdered him when she died
He didn't know how he'd survive
Women he dated were vultures
Wanting money, not love
But their words were sweet as toffee
They cajoled him, told him he was funny
At home, he grabbed a bottle, took a swig
The drink was his best friend
In his mind, it made him see sense
He lay in bed and wept
Sleeping, waking to do it all again

Hope and fear stole my heart
Now I lived at home
Watched over by Dad
I was a slave, baking, and washing
Tending to the farm animals, saying nothing
Frightened about making a mistake
I cannot sacrifice my life to be a wife and mother
I'd rather live alone in a bubble
At least I'll cause no more trouble
When God meets me in Paradise
He'll forgive the things I've done wrong
That was what the priest said

My hands kept busy knitting
Needles clacking, making a jumper
My fingers were aching
I was supposed to be healing,
Mending my heart and mind
But I felt like a mistake in the wool
Unraveling, until there was nothing left,
But one straight line
I started again
The cat pounced, thinking it was a game
Her paws stroked and clawed
The wool shredded
And I couldn't be mended anymore
I was like a person on a deserted island
Marking a tree each day
Mum and my love were away
But there was nothing tropical
I wasn't on a holiday
The wool was my lifeline
To my yesterdays, today, and tomorrow
And the emptiness I felt within

The clock in the hallway chimed ten
The front door closed,
I was alone again
Dad was dating the same woman
She wore black clothes and black shoes
I wondered if she was in mourning too
The telephone rang out in the hall
My life had become a bore
I was a cobra ready to strike
Engulfed in my venom

Desires filtered through my brain
Like a rainbow after the rain
Memories rose from years gone by
About hopes, cares, and dreams
That have made me who I am today
Errors did abound, making an unearthly sound
Like a volcano erupting out at sea,
The pain I caused, I did regret
Even though at the time
I thought I'd done my best
But I knew I had caused a lot of misery

Warm tears burst
From my tremulous eyes
While viewing a video,
Evelyn's new parents had sent
My lips quivered like wind blowing
Over a creek bed
Evelyn smiled brightly as the sun
Even though her fragile limbs
Told otherwise, and she fell
In front of them
They picked her up, and she tottered
Squealing with glee,
Whisked up in her new mother's arms
Her first steps on earth
I didn't get to see

***

Dad appeared in the doorway
Weak and grey
Inquisitive eyes like a child
Wanting a better day
Feet moving up and down
Fumbling with his hands,
Unable to remember
Current things
His brain locked in memories
The joy and sadness that they'd bring
Silly smile upon his face
Once a proud man
Now he needed his nappy changed
I clothed and fed him
Until the day he died
Now I live alone
Listening to the house creak and groan
The animals are my friends
For which I still attend

My feet walked
The earth with calm
When the rains came
It was like a cleansing balm
Beyond my eyes
Love did lie
For other people, still not I
Every year I visited the river
Peering at my image, mirroring me,
Giving me wrinkles, making me shudder
At other times, appearing serene
Over time, I had changed in its eyes
I was young, now I am old
This year, the river disappeared
No longer fathomless
Like our love,
The sun was a fire
That once fueled our passion
Now the landscape was cracked and ravaged
I no longer knew what people saw
When they looked at me
The river raged on in my heart and mind
Reflecting on all that had been

Over the years,
My mind wandered to our child
What would she look like now?
If we did meet
Would I recognize her?
My eyes blurred
I'd be frightened her scorn
And outrage would be unrelenting
When all I'd want to tell her
Was how much she was loved
I'm sorry she was taken away
I had no say in anything that day
Please believe me,
I come as a friend, not a foe
The mere thought of it
Sent my heart full of woe
There was no joy in my error
All I'd experienced was
Unrest and terror
She had lived because
Of our pleasure in my youth
That was my solemn truth
My foolish pride in believing
I knew everything
When my parents had known better,
I was sure my love
Would've made a good father
And now watched over her from heaven
I conjured an image of our child
With gentle green eyes, long flowing

Auburn hair, bronzed complexion
Tall and thin
But I refused to acknowledge
She was better off with people
That were not her blood
I hope she forgave me
For what my parents had done

No one tended to me in times of distress
I woke, worked, and slept
My memory faded as I grew old
My eyes wore glasses
So, I could thread a needle
To mend my clothes
I was invisible to farmers
Young and old
Faint limbs bent
Working on the dusty plain
Wondering if I'd see anyone again
Walking with God in my heart and mind
He was the only solace I could find

I was a flower
My seeds germinated
Rose out of the earth
Blooming with dry roots,
Shaking stem
Breathing in fear,
Standing resolute
Scorched by the sun
Day-after-day
I bowed my head and prayed
Nobody listened
They'd all gone away
To a better place
One petal left
Holding on tight
A cloud burst opened
Pouring rain
But it was too late
I fell over
Like Mum and died
Without anyone around
To say goodbye

www.ingramcontent.com/pod-product-compliance
Lightning Source LLC
Chambersburg PA
CBHW071717040426
42446CB00011B/2110